MW01248127

The Deadly Shooting of Brian Thompson

How Luigi Mangione Became a Symbol of America's Battle Against Unfair Healthcare Practices

LINDSEY T. GORDON

The Deadly Shooting of Brian Thompson

COPYRIGHT

The Deadly Shooting of Brian Thompson

TABLE OF CONTENTS

INTRODUCTION..........................**8**

The Catalyst for Tragedy:
Understanding the Context....................8

Who Was Brian Thompson? A
Look at the Victim........................... 12

The Rise of Luigi Mangione: The
Man Behind the Tragedy...................15

CHAPTER ONE........................... **21**

The Day That Changed
Everything........................... 21

The Morning of December 4,
2023.................................... 22

The Assassination: How It
Unfolded...........................25

Witness Accounts and Initial
Reactions...........................28

CHAPTER TWO...........................**34**

The Manhunt and Capture of Luigi
Mangione............................... 34

The Search Begins: A Nationwide
Manhunt...........................35

The Deadly Shooting of Brian Thompson

Mangione's Final Stand in
Pennsylvania.....................................39
The Capture: From McDonald's
to Extradition...................................44
CHAPTER THREE..........................48
The Courtroom Drama: State-Level
Charges... 48
Mangione's Plea and the Legal
Proceedings......................................49
The Charges: Murder and
Terrorism Explained........................54
Reactions in Court: Defiance and
Smiles Amidst Tragedy.................... 59
CHAPTER FOUR............................ 64
The Federal Charges: Stalking,
Murder, and Healthcare
Grievances....................................... 64
The Role of Federal
Prosecutors..................................... 66
Accusations of Hostility Towards
the Healthcare System.....................70
The Implications of Federal
Charges on the Legal
Outcome.. 75

CHAPTER FIVE............................ **80**

Healthcare in America: The Roots
of Discontent... 80

    The High Cost of Healthcare in
    the U.S...82

    Denied Claims and the Strain on
    Families...86

    The Role of Health Insurance
    Companies in Public Anger...............91

CHAPTER SIX.............................. **97**

Luigi Mangione's Motive: More
Than a Murder...................................... 97

    The Personal Grievance Against
    UnitedHealthcare............................. 99

    The Writing Found in
    Mangione's Notebook...................... 103

    Understanding His View on the
    Healthcare System.......................... 107

CHAPTER SEVEN........................ **112**

Public Perception: From Villain to
Folk Hero..112

    The Supporters Who Gathered
    Outside the Court............................114

The Role of Social Media in Glorifying Mangione......................118

The Tactics Behind the "Free Luigi" Movement...........................121

CHAPTER EIGHT....................**127**

The Protest Movement: Healthcare Reform in the Spotlight.....................127

The Rallying Cry for Healthcare Justice......................................129

Voices of the Oppressed: Testimonials from Protesters..........133

How the Shooting Sparked a Nationwide Debate.........................137

CHAPTER NINE....................**143**

Brian Thompson's Legacy: A Father's Impact...............................143

The Life and Career of Brian Thompson...................................144

Thompson's Role at UnitedHealthcare.........................148

The Impact of His Death on His Family and the Healthcare Industry......................................153

CHAPTER TEN............................ **158**

The Larger Implications:
Terrorism, Politics, and
Healthcare...158

The Definition of Terrorism in
Mangione's Case..............................159

Healthcare Policy Reform:
What's Next?................................... 163

Legal Precedents and How This
Case Could Reshape Future
Prosecutions...................................168

CONCLUSION.............................**173**

Reflection on the Tragedy and Its
Consequences.......................................173

Moving Forward: The Fight for
Healthcare Justice........................... 177

The Continuing Debate: Can
True Change Come from
Violence?.. **181**

INTRODUCTION

The Catalyst for Tragedy: Understanding the Context

The tragic and shocking murder of Brian Thompson, the CEO of UnitedHealthcare, on December 4, 2023, sent waves of disbelief and horror throughout the United States. The brutality of the crime was compounded by the fact that the perpetrator, 26-year-old Luigi Mangione, was not just a killer but also a symbol of widespread anger and frustration against the American healthcare system.

This introduction seeks to lay the foundation for understanding the underlying causes that led to this violent act, the life and legacy of the victim, and the rise of Mangione as a figure intertwined with national debates about healthcare.

To comprehend the significance of this tragic event, we must first examine the broader societal context that made it not just a personal vendetta, but also a reflection of widespread frustrations with the American healthcare system.

For decades, the U.S. has struggled with an undercurrent of discontent regarding the high costs of healthcare, the pervasive power of health insurance companies, and the inequities in coverage that many Americans face. Rising premiums, deductibles, and out-of-pocket expenses, along with the constant struggle for approval of medical treatments, have pushed many to their limits.

Health insurers, such as UnitedHealthcare, one of the largest and most influential companies in the industry, have been at the center of these grievances. Critics argue that these companies routinely deny claims, delay treatments, or refuse to cover necessary procedures, putting millions of Americans at risk and forcing them to bear the financial burden of their own health care.

This creates a system in which the insured, often already struggling with medical issues, are further burdened by mounting debts and denied claims, which only fuels anger and resentment.

The growing gap between the wealthy executives at the top of these insurance giants and the individuals whose lives are impacted by their policies is a significant source of tension.

The attack on Brian Thompson, who had been at the helm of UnitedHealthcare for several years, was not an isolated incident. It was the culmination of years of escalating resentment towards a system perceived as prioritizing profit over people's well-being.

While Mangione's actions were extreme, they can be seen as part of a broader wave of discontentment and growing anger directed at the entrenched powers of the healthcare industry.

The Deadly Shooting of Brian Thompson

Who Was Brian Thompson? A Look at the Victim

Brian Thompson was not just the CEO of UnitedHealthcare; he was a father, a colleague, and a leader within the healthcare industry. Thompson had worked in various executive roles throughout his career and had taken charge of UnitedHealthcare, one of the largest health insurers in the U.S., in recent years.

Under his leadership, the company had grown to have an even more dominant presence in the healthcare space, but with that growth came increasing scrutiny from critics who accused the company of contributing to the growing healthcare crisis in America.

The Deadly Shooting of Brian Thompson

Thompson was a complex individual, admired by many for his sharp business acumen, yet criticized by others for his role in an industry that was often seen as a profit-driven enterprise with little regard for the individuals it served.

For many, Thompson symbolized the upper echelon of the healthcare industry—one that benefited from rising premiums while leaving patients to face the devastating consequences of denied claims and rising medical costs. He had been involved in multiple initiatives aimed at reforming healthcare, but these efforts were often overshadowed by the more controversial aspects of the company's operations.

The Deadly Shooting of Brian Thompson

Brian Thompson's death, therefore, became symbolic not just because he was a high-profile figure, but also because of what he represented: the system that millions of Americans had come to view as unjust, profit-driven, and unfeeling.

His assassination shook the industry and the nation, not just because of the manner of his death, but because it was a stark reminder of how deeply entrenched the resentment towards healthcare companies had become.

Thompson's death left behind a family, including two children, who now must grapple with the sudden loss of a father and husband. For them, the tragedy was not just an abstract political statement but a personal and deeply painful event that has left scars that will never heal.

The Rise of Luigi Mangione: The Man Behind the Tragedy

The name Luigi Mangione would soon become known across the country, but his rise to infamy is rooted in a deeply personal story of disillusionment and anger. A 26-year-old from a modest background, Mangione had lived much of his life in the shadow of the American healthcare system.

For him, healthcare wasn't just an abstract issue—it was a source of personal suffering. Mangione had witnessed firsthand the devastating impact that denied insurance claims could have on a family.

His own mother had faced significant health struggles that were complicated by delays and denials of coverage. Like many Americans, Mangione's family had been trapped in the cycle of trying to navigate the complex and often impenetrable healthcare bureaucracy.

In the months leading up to the murder, Mangione's grievances with the healthcare system appeared to deepen. His frustrations were amplified by the experience of watching loved ones suffer under a system that seemed more concerned with profits than with people's lives.

According to reports, Mangione had become fixated on the idea of revenge against those he believed were responsible for the widespread suffering caused by health insurers like UnitedHealthcare.

Mangione's anger was not just directed at the companies themselves but at the individuals who led them—people like Brian Thompson, who he saw as the face of an oppressive system.

The personal animosity he harbored toward Thompson was likely compounded by his belief that Thompson, as the CEO of one of the largest health insurance companies in the country, was directly responsible for the suffering that had touched his own life and the lives of countless others.

His feelings of powerlessness in the face of an industry he believed was indifferent to human suffering may have fueled his decision to take matters into his own hands. Mangione's actions on that fateful morning in Manhattan were not just the result of an isolated incident but the culmination of years of pent-up frustration with a system that had failed him and many others.

His criminal act, while tragic, also underscored the extent to which some individuals had become radicalized by their experiences with an unjust healthcare system.

In the aftermath of the shooting, Mangione's supporters, some of whom had suffered similar personal losses, began to view him not as a criminal, but as a symbol of defiance against the power of health insurance companies.

While his actions were undeniably extreme, they struck a chord with a public that was growing increasingly weary of rising healthcare costs and the relentless influence of insurance companies. Mangione became, for some, an unlikely folk hero—a martyr in a war against a system many viewed as broken.

The story of Luigi Mangione is not one of simple criminality, but of a man whose personal suffering and growing frustration with an unjust system ultimately led him to take drastic, violent action.

The Deadly Shooting of Brian Thompson

His rise from an ordinary individual to a symbol of rebellion against the healthcare industry is a chilling reflection of the deep-seated issues that persist in America's healthcare system today.

CHAPTER ONE

The Day That Changed Everything

The tragedy that unfolded on the morning of December 4, 2023, in the heart of Manhattan was not just another violent incident in a city known for its bustling streets and occasional outbursts of chaos.

This was an assassination that would forever alter the course of the healthcare debate in America, sending shockwaves through the public and leaving a trail of unanswered questions. The murder of Brian Thompson, the CEO of UnitedHealthcare, was a horrifying moment in time that would forever be associated with one man's rage and the intense national conversation about the failures of the U.S. healthcare system.

The Morning of December 4, 2023

It was a cold, brisk December morning in New York City. The usual hustle of commuters made their way to work, the sidewalks packed with people heading to business meetings, coffee shops, and train stations.

In the midst of this, Brian Thompson, the highly regarded CEO of UnitedHealthcare, was making his way to a major investor conference in Manhattan, a key event that had attracted top figures from the healthcare and finance sectors. Thompson, dressed in his usual professional attire—a dark suit and tie—walked down the streets near Times Square with a sense of purpose.

The Deadly Shooting of Brian Thompson

At that moment, Thompson appeared to be just another corporate executive going about his day, unaware of the danger lurking ahead. It was shortly before 9 a.m. when the first signs of something deeply tragic began to unfold. As Thompson walked along a relatively quiet stretch of 7th Avenue, just a block away from his destination, he was suddenly approached by a lone figure.

Luigi Mangione, who had been carefully watching Thompson for days, was positioned in the crowd, blending in with the other passersby. His eyes fixed on the man he had come to see as the symbol of all the injustice he had experienced at the hands of healthcare insurers.

The Deadly Shooting of Brian Thompson

With a cold precision, Mangione stepped forward, pulled a concealed handgun from under his coat, and fired. The first shot rang out, striking Thompson in the back. Before Thompson could react or flee, a second shot found its mark, this time in the head, killing him instantly.

Mangione, after completing the act, calmly lowered the gun and walked away. He did not flee immediately, taking a deliberate few moments to ensure that his target was no longer alive. As he walked down the street, people around him were frozen in shock.

A few witnesses later recounted the moment as surreal, with many assuming the shots were part of some kind of terrorist attack or an accident in the chaos of the crowded city streets. Little did they know that this was a calculated assassination aimed directly at one of the most powerful men in the U.S. healthcare system.

The Assassination: How It Unfolded

The unfolding of Brian Thompson's assassination was a tragic series of events that happened so quickly it left little time for any real response. The first shot was fired at 8:52 a.m., and the second followed just moments later. In the early seconds after the gunshots rang out, pedestrians nearby reacted with disbelief.

One woman, who had been walking a few feet ahead of Thompson, turned to see him collapse onto the sidewalk, blood pooling beneath his head. She screamed for help, causing several people to run for cover and others to pull out their phones to document the scene.

At first, it seemed as though the gunman might still be nearby, as bystanders scrambled to safety, thinking there could be more danger lurking. But in the chaos, Mangione managed to remain undetected as he moved into the crowd. The New York City streets, busy with pedestrians, had turned into a chaotic scene of confusion and fear.

Emergency services were alerted almost immediately, but the speed of the attack had left little opportunity for intervention. By the time paramedics arrived on the scene, Thompson had already been pronounced dead from his injuries.

Police quickly cordoned off the area, searching for any potential witnesses who could provide further details about the suspect. As the investigation unfolded, detectives pieced together a chilling picture of premeditation.

Mangione had been following Thompson's movements for several days, carefully planning the location and timing of the assassination to maximize impact and minimize the chance of being caught.

The fact that Mangione had not just attacked Thompson, but did so in such a public, calculated manner, pointed to a deep level of conviction and anger directed at the healthcare executive and the industry he represented.

Witness Accounts and Initial Reactions

The witnesses who were in close proximity to the assassination were left traumatized by the events they had just witnessed. Many described the scene as surreal, with people not knowing how to react as gunshots echoed through the street.

One woman, who had been walking directly behind Thompson, recalled hearing two sharp cracks before she saw him collapse. "It was like time stopped for a moment," she said. "I couldn't believe what I was seeing. It just didn't feel real." Other witnesses described seeing Mangione walking calmly after the shots were fired, which only added to the chilling nature of the attack.

The Deadly Shooting of Brian Thompson

Police officers who were the first to respond reported a scene of pandemonium. With New York City being a hub of daily life and routine, it took only moments for the incident to become headline news, and the street where Thompson had been killed quickly became a crime scene, surrounded by reporters and concerned citizens trying to piece together what had happened.

As the news spread, initial reactions were varied. The media was quick to report the incident, but many were unclear about the motive behind the assassination. At first, law enforcement speculated that it could have been a random act of violence or a robbery gone wrong. However, as investigators began to analyze the details—witness testimonies, surveillance footage, and Mangione's previous activities—it became apparent that this was a targeted killing.

In the days following the assassination, the country was engulfed in a mixture of shock, disbelief, and, for some, a sense of uneasy understanding. Thompson's murder sparked a nationwide conversation about healthcare, particularly the role of insurance companies in shaping policy and denying coverage. For some, the act was seen as an expression of profound frustration with an industry that seemed to operate beyond the reach of accountability.

While law enforcement and the media tried to uncover the true motivations behind Mangione's actions, the reaction from the public was polarized. Many expressed horror at the murder of a man who was, in their eyes, simply doing his job, while others saw Thompson as a representation of the very system they had come to despise.

The conversation quickly moved beyond the details of the crime itself to the larger issues it symbolized—the failures of the American healthcare system and the extreme lengths to which some individuals might go to express their anger and desperation.

The reactions to the shooting were not just limited to the public but also extended to the healthcare industry, which now found itself thrust into a brutal spotlight. UnitedHealthcare, as well as other major insurance providers, had long been under fire for policies that many believed were designed to maximize profits at the expense of patient care.

The assassination, while tragic, highlighted the simmering resentment against these practices and drew attention to the desperate need for reform in a system that, for many, had become increasingly opaque, complex, and harmful.

For those who supported Mangione's views, Thompson's death was seen as a grotesque but necessary jolt to the conversation about healthcare reform—a conversation that had been desperately needed for years but had often been ignored or downplayed by policymakers and corporate executives.

The act of violence would, however, serve as a tragic reminder of just how deep the divisions had become, and how personal and widespread the frustrations had grown.

CHAPTER TWO

The Manhunt and Capture of Luigi Mangione

In the immediate aftermath of Brian Thompson's assassination, authorities began a swift and intense search for Luigi Mangione, the man believed to have executed the high-profile murder. What followed was not just a typical manhunt but a nationwide pursuit that captured the attention of both law enforcement and the public.

The hunt for Mangione was complicated by the fact that he was considered both highly dangerous and unpredictable, and the scope of the search extended beyond just New York City. His capture would take days, leading to an intense final confrontation in a fast-food restaurant in Pennsylvania.

The details of Mangione's flight from justice, his brief and tense standoff with law enforcement, and his eventual extradition to New York would become a crucial part of the narrative surrounding this tragic event.

The Search Begins: A Nationwide Manhunt

The moment the gunshots rang out on December 4, 2023, and Brian Thompson collapsed to the pavement, law enforcement in New York City immediately launched an investigation. Within hours, police had pieced together the basic facts of the crime: a targeted killing of one of the most powerful men in the healthcare industry.

The Deadly Shooting of Brian Thompson

While the initial focus was on identifying the suspect and gathering evidence from the crime scene, the realization soon dawned that the man responsible had vanished without a trace, blending into the crowded streets of Manhattan before slipping away entirely.

Detectives initially believed that Mangione, being so young and unfamiliar with the complexities of evading capture, would not have gotten far. However, as hours turned into days, it became clear that the suspect was far more organized and determined than they had anticipated.

Security footage from nearby cameras, combined with witness descriptions, helped to sketch a general outline of Mangione's appearance and movements, but there was still no indication of his whereabouts. His motivations had quickly become a focal point of the investigation, but the priority was to catch him before he could flee the city.

As the manhunt expanded, law enforcement issued a nationwide alert, with the FBI and local police forces across multiple states coordinating efforts. Mangione's identity was confirmed, and a photo of him was released to the public, along with details of the crime.

Authorities quickly began to track down any leads that might point to his next move. In an era where fugitives often seek to leave the country or disappear into hiding, investigators had to account for the possibility that Mangione could attempt to flee the United States altogether.

Every crossing, airport, and highway exit was closely monitored as police worked to piece together any pattern of behavior that could hint at Mangione's direction.

The search didn't just involve the traditional methods of law enforcement but also leveraged modern technology. The FBI tracked his digital footprint, combing through bank records, credit card transactions, and social media activity in search of a clue that might lead to his whereabouts. They scoured phone records for any calls or messages that might indicate where Mangione had gone.

His past social interactions, from his workplace to acquaintances and online contacts, were analyzed in depth.

The breakthrough came when a tip-off revealed that Mangione had been using an alias at a small motel just outside New York City, but by the time authorities arrived, he had already fled. As days passed, the search widened. Law enforcement's focus shifted to nearby states, hoping to follow the trail of the fugitive who was determined to evade capture.

Mangione's Final Stand in Pennsylvania

After several days of relentless pursuit, the manhunt finally reached its dramatic climax on December 9, 2023. Luigi Mangione, a fugitive now on the run for almost a week, found himself cornered in a small town in Pennsylvania, several hundred miles from New York City.

The search had taken law enforcement officers across several states, from New Jersey to Maryland, but it was a tip-off from a local resident that would lead them to the fast-food restaurant where Mangione was hiding.

At a McDonald's in the small town of Allentown, Pennsylvania, Mangione had entered the restaurant to grab a quick meal, assuming that he would remain undetected. It was a decision that would prove to be his downfall. He had been using a fake identity throughout his time on the run, changing his appearance slightly and trying to keep a low profile, but his time in hiding was running out.

Authorities, by this point, had received a tip from someone who had recognized him from the public alerts. The tip-off was key in narrowing down his location.

When law enforcement arrived at the McDonald's, they were able to confirm that Mangione was indeed inside. They surrounded the restaurant, effectively trapping him within the building. Inside, Mangione was unaware that he was about to be apprehended. Surveillance footage would later reveal that Mangione appeared calm, even oblivious to the fact that the noose was tightening around him.

He ordered food and sat down to eat, trying to blend in as if he were simply a regular customer. But outside, a team of FBI agents, local law enforcement, and SWAT officers were positioning themselves for the confrontation.

The tense moments that followed would become an intense standoff, but Mangione's luck had finally run out. Just before 2 p.m. that afternoon, a tactical team stormed the McDonald's, and Mangione was arrested without further incident.

He was found sitting alone at a booth, holding a fast-food bag in his lap. The arrest was remarkably calm, considering the circumstances, as Mangione was taken into custody with no resistance.

A search of his person revealed a gun matching the weapon used in Thompson's assassination, as well as a fake ID.

The brief period of his evasion was over. The culmination of a manhunt that spanned nearly a week had led law enforcement directly to Mangione, and his final act of defiance was met with swift justice. Mangione was detained and handcuffed without incident and, remarkably, was not combative during the arrest.

At the time of his capture, authorities noted that he appeared tired and disheveled, but otherwise composed, as though he had been preparing for the inevitable end of his flight from the law.

The Capture: From McDonald's to Extradition

Once Mangione was arrested, the process of extraditing him back to New York City began immediately. Pennsylvania police held him for questioning, but law enforcement officials in New York City were eager to bring him back to face charges for the assassination of Brian Thompson. Given the seriousness of the charges, which included multiple counts of murder, terrorism, and stalking, Mangione was treated as a high-profile detainee.

During the early stages of his arrest, Mangione remained largely silent, providing little in terms of a defense or explanation for his actions. He was placed in a secure holding facility in Pennsylvania, where he was kept under tight surveillance while awaiting the legal process that would eventually lead to his transfer.

The authorities in New York City made it clear that they would not let Mangione escape the long arm of the law, and arrangements were made for his transfer.

On December 12, 2023, just days after his arrest, Mangione was flown back to New York City under heavy guard. He was transported in a federal convoy, and upon arrival at the Brooklyn Federal Detention Center, he was processed and taken into custody.

Media outlets across the country were watching closely, and Mangione's capture marked a pivotal moment in the case, though it was only the beginning of the legal and political fallout that would follow.

As Mangione was officially extradited and moved into the hands of New York authorities, the public attention turned to his upcoming trials. While his supporters painted him as a martyr for healthcare reform, the legal system would need to determine whether his actions were driven by ideological beliefs or whether he was simply a man who had taken violent and extreme measures to address his grievances.

His capture, as much as it brought relief to the law enforcement community, also brought new questions to the surface—about the nature of his actions, his motives, and the consequences of living in a society where deep frustration with systems of power could lead to violent outbursts.

The saga of Luigi Mangione, from his assassination of Brian Thompson to his eventual capture, was far from over, but the days of his flight were now a dark chapter in the unfolding story of one man's war against the American healthcare system.

CHAPTER THREE

The Courtroom Drama: State-Level Charges

The capture of Luigi Mangione in Pennsylvania marked just the beginning of the legal drama that would unfold over the next several months. Once in custody, Mangione faced a long and complex judicial process, with his case dividing public opinion and sparking fierce debates on both the legality of his actions and the underlying causes of the violence.

As the prosecution moved forward with state-level charges, Mangione's legal team worked to defend him, setting the stage for a courtroom spectacle that would captivate the nation.

This chapter will delve into the emotional and legal battle that took place in the courtroom, the charges Mangione faced, and the conflicting reactions from both the legal community and the public.

Mangione's Plea and the Legal Proceedings

On December 18, 2023, just two weeks after his arrest, Mangione was brought into the courtroom of the Manhattan Supreme Court for his arraignment. The courtroom, usually reserved for less sensational cases, was packed with reporters, legal professionals, and a small group of supporters who had gathered to show their allegiance to the defendant. The anticipation in the room was palpable, as this was the first time Mangione would face charges for the murder of Brian

The Deadly Shooting of Brian Thompson

Thompson and the subsequent terror attack he had committed.

Mangione appeared before Judge Rachel Walker, shackled at the ankles and wrists, and was seated next to his defense attorney, who would later become a central figure in the case.

The charges against him were read aloud: eleven counts of murder, including murder as an act of terrorism, as well as multiple counts of stalking, illegal possession of firearms, and harassment. When asked to enter his plea, Mangione's voice was calm and measured. He pleaded not guilty to all charges.

The plea set the stage for a lengthy trial, one that would likely involve high-stakes arguments over mental health, political motivations, and the legality of his actions.

In the courtroom, Mangione maintained a composed demeanor, occasionally whispering to his legal team but offering little else in terms of emotion. His refusal to express remorse or regret over the killing raised eyebrows and would play a significant role in shaping the public's perception of him.

The legal proceedings in the early stages of the case revolved around the preliminary hearing, during which the prosecution outlined its case against Mangione. Prosecutors painted a vivid picture of the events leading up to the murder, highlighting the chilling premeditation involved.

They referenced evidence that showed Mangione had been stalking Thompson for weeks, gathering information on his routines, and even sending disturbing messages on social media about his disdain for the healthcare industry.

Mangione's defense team, led by the experienced criminal attorney Anthony Miller, argued that their client's actions were driven by a deep sense of frustration with the healthcare system, but they also claimed that Mangione suffered from severe mental health issues, including a history of untreated depression and paranoia.

They proposed that the crime was not simply one of calculated violence but the result of an individual who had lost touch with reality after years of struggling to navigate the system he viewed as unfair and oppressive.

The prosecution's case rested heavily on the assertion that Mangione's murder of Thompson was an act of terrorism—an ideological assassination intended to send a message to the healthcare industry. The defense, meanwhile, emphasized that Mangione was an individual who had been radicalized by the overwhelming sense of injustice he felt, and that his actions, while tragic, were symptomatic of a larger societal problem.

The trial was not expected to be swift, given the complexity of the charges and the potential for an extended legal battle over Mangione's mental state and motives.

The Charges: Murder and Terrorism Explained

The charges against Mangione were not only severe but also unusual, given the political undertones of the crime. While murder cases in the United States often involve personal motives such as jealousy, rage, or revenge, the circumstances surrounding Thompson's death had introduced a chilling new element to the case—terrorism.

Under New York State law, murder can be classified as either first-degree or second-degree, depending on the circumstances.

First-degree murder typically involves premeditation and malice aforethought, while second-degree murder may occur without prior planning but still involves intent to kill. However, Mangione's actions were escalated due to the prosecution's classification of the killing as an act of terrorism, a legal charge that carries significantly harsher penalties.

The legal definition of terrorism in this case was critical to understanding the gravity of Mangione's charges. Prosecutors argued that the murder was not just a crime of passion or personal vendetta but an intentional act designed to strike fear into the public and bring attention to a political cause—the reform of the American healthcare system.

They pointed to the specific language found in a notebook that Mangione had written in prior to the shooting, which contained hostile references to the healthcare industry and wealthy executives.

Additionally, the fact that the murder took place in a public space—on a crowded street in Manhattan—served to underscore the terroristic nature of the act. The goal, prosecutors contended, was to send a message to the powerful figures in the healthcare industry and intimidate them into action.

The charges of terrorism were particularly contentious, as the legal community debated whether the case truly fit the definition of a terrorist act. Legal experts pointed out that terrorism charges were usually reserved for individuals or groups who committed acts of violence to influence government policy or instill fear on a larger scale, often tied to political or ideological movements.

In this case, Mangione's target was a corporate executive, not a government official, and while his actions may have been politically motivated, some questioned whether they qualified as terrorism in a strict legal sense.

Despite these debates, the jury would ultimately have to decide whether

Mangione's actions rose to the level of terrorism. The defense, on the other hand, argued that labeling the crime as terrorism was an overreach, a way for the prosecution to increase the severity of the charges and ensure a harsher punishment.

They contended that while Mangione's actions were undeniably violent and tragic, they were driven by personal grievances with the healthcare industry rather than a larger, organized movement aimed at destabilizing the government.

The legal experts were divided over the outcome of these charges, with some speculating that Mangione might be convicted on lesser charges of second-degree murder and aggravated assault, but others fearing that the terrorism charge would stick, dramatically increasing his potential sentence.

Reactions in Court: Defiance and Smiles Amidst Tragedy

Throughout the initial hearings, Mangione's demeanor in the courtroom was as captivating as it was unsettling. While many of the observers expected him to show signs of remorse or guilt, Mangione's behavior often left the courtroom stunned. He appeared calm, almost detached, as he sat next to his defense attorney.

He spoke little during the proceedings, occasionally whispering to his lawyer, but otherwise maintained an impassive expression.

The Deadly Shooting of Brian Thompson

At times, he even smiled—especially when interacting with his legal team—an action that struck many in the courtroom as deeply inappropriate given the gravity of the charges against him.

Some of the families of those affected by Thompson's death found Mangione's apparent lack of remorse disturbing. They had come to the courtroom in the hopes of seeing a man who had at least some understanding of the pain he had caused, but instead, they were confronted with a defendant who seemed unshaken by the murder of a father of two.

The prosecution noted this demeanor as indicative of Mangione's deep ideological commitment to his cause, suggesting that his actions were not an act of passion or anger but rather the culmination of a long-standing political struggle.

On the other hand, Mangione's supporters outside the courthouse interpreted his behavior differently. A small group of protesters had gathered during the trial, holding placards and chanting slogans such as "Free Luigi" and "Healthcare is a right, not a privilege."

For them, Mangione was a hero—a man who had struck a blow against a corrupt and unjust system. They saw his smiling and composed demeanor as a sign of strength and defiance in the face of a system that had failed so many people like them.

One supporter, who had lost his mother to denied insurance claims, told reporters, "Mangione is not a killer. He's a martyr for all of us who have been crushed under the weight of this insurance machine. He did what none of us could do." This division in public opinion would only intensify as the trial progressed, making Mangione a figure of intense emotional and ideological debate.

Inside the courtroom, the reactions were mixed. Some legal analysts noted that Mangione's behavior, while unusual, was consistent with a person who had come to view himself as a symbol of a cause greater than himself.

His refusal to express remorse or regret could be seen as an indication of his belief in the righteousness of his actions—an unsettling trait for those hoping for any form of accountability or justice. The trial, in its early stages, was a battleground not just for the facts of the case but for the soul of the justice system itself.

CHAPTER FOUR

The Federal Charges: Stalking, Murder, and Healthcare Grievances

While Luigi Mangione's state-level trial focused on his actions within New York, his legal battles did not end there. In addition to the murder and terrorism charges he faced at the state level, federal prosecutors swiftly moved forward with their own case, adding a layer of complexity and severity to the already high-profile case.

The federal charges against Mangione were deeply rooted in his alleged hostility towards the healthcare system and its powerful figures, notably his victim, Brian Thompson. These charges not only expanded the scope of his alleged crimes but also brought forward a set of legal consequences that would significantly impact his overall fate.

Federal prosecutors aimed to ensure that Mangione was held accountable for his actions under a set of national laws that dealt with interstate criminal activity, stalking, and violent acts carried out with clear ideological motivations. The federal case would delve deeper into Mangione's personal grievances with healthcare executives and his apparent obsession with the issues that led to Thompson's murder.

This chapter will explore the nature of the federal charges against Mangione, the specific allegations of stalking and violence, and the broader implications of these federal charges on the outcome of his legal battles.

The Role of Federal Prosecutors

The federal case against Mangione was initiated shortly after his arrest, and it became clear that prosecutors would pursue the charges with full force. Unlike state-level charges, federal prosecutors had access to a broader array of legal tools and resources.

Federal involvement in the case was crucial given the nature of the crimes—especially considering the cross-state elements of Mangione's movements before his arrest in Pennsylvania, as well as his apparent nationwide fixation on the healthcare industry.

Federal prosecutors, led by U.S. Attorney for the Southern District of New York, Rachel Levitt, took a stern approach to the case. They noted that Mangione's actions were not just about personal revenge but also about sending a message on a larger scale. The federal charges included stalking, interstate murder, and violations of federal gun laws.

These charges were particularly alarming because they suggested that Mangione's grievances with the healthcare system went far beyond just one individual. His crime, they argued, was part of a larger, calculated attack on a powerful industry that he perceived as being corrupt and unjust.

The federal case had the power to carry much harsher penalties, especially given that Mangione was charged with murder across state lines—making it an interstate crime.

The federal government also had a vested interest in framing the case as one that was about domestic terrorism, with Mangione's act of violence falling under the scope of crimes motivated by political, social, or ideological beliefs. This would allow federal prosecutors to push for a longer sentence, potentially life in prison, and to position the case as a warning against similar acts of violence targeting powerful institutions.

Federal prosecutors used several key pieces of evidence to build their case. Notably, a notebook discovered at the time of Mangione's arrest contained several pages filled with detailed thoughts, writings, and observations that clearly outlined his disdain for the healthcare industry.

The notebook offered a window into Mangione's psyche and helped prosecutors establish that his crime was premeditated and ideologically motivated, further bolstering the argument that his actions were terrorist in nature.

One of the most critical pieces of evidence in the federal case was Mangione's communication with various social media platforms, in which he posted content that criticized the healthcare industry, calling for drastic reforms and, in some instances, threatening specific figures within the industry.

These messages were traced back to his accounts and linked to his pattern of stalking and harassment, offering further proof of the personal and ideological nature of his crimes.

Accusations of Hostility Towards the Healthcare System

At the core of the federal charges was Mangione's intense, and often vocal, hostility towards the healthcare system in the United States. Federal prosecutors worked to demonstrate that the defendant was not merely an individual with a personal vendetta against Brian Thompson but someone who had cultivated a broader animus toward the entire healthcare system and its corporate elites.

This animosity was seen as central to understanding his decision to kill Thompson, a figurehead of one of the largest health insurance companies in the world.

According to federal investigators, Mangione had been researching Thompson for weeks before the murder. He had gathered personal information about the UnitedHealthcare CEO's daily routine, and even looked into his company's policies and dealings.

Mangione's frustration seemed to stem from years of personal experiences with insurance claims being denied, an ongoing theme in his writings and public commentary. He had become obsessed with the idea that insurance companies were systematically denying coverage to vulnerable people in order to maximize profits.

This obsession was exacerbated by Mangione's own battles with the healthcare system, which he believed had not only failed him but had ruined the lives of countless others.

In his writings, Mangione often described what he perceived as a moral obligation to take action against an industry he viewed as predatory. He believed that healthcare executives like Brian Thompson represented the "greed and callousness" of the corporate elite, and that violent retribution was the only way to force systemic change.

This intense hostility was reflected in the choice of Thompson as a target. Prosecutors argued that the murder was not just a random act of violence but a deliberate strike against the symbol of an entire system that Mangione had come to despise.

One of the most chilling aspects of Mangione's motivations, as revealed through his communications and his arrest notes, was his belief that the healthcare system was responsible for countless deaths. In several online posts, he had referred to people who died from preventable conditions as victims of the system.

Mangione felt that healthcare companies—like UnitedHealthcare, with its vast financial resources—were directly responsible for the suffering of millions of Americans who could not afford or access the care they needed. He even suggested in one message that the only way to stop the greed and "unchecked power" of these companies was through radical action.

Mangione's narrative painted the healthcare system as an antagonist, a faceless villain that had to be confronted with force. This ideology, mixed with his growing personal grievances, turned his frustration into a lethal mission.

Federal prosecutors emphasized that Mangione's writings were not the rants of an isolated individual but the mindset of someone who had been radicalized by the very systems he aimed to dismantle.

The Implications of Federal Charges on the Legal Outcome

The federal charges against Mangione had significant implications for both his defense strategy and the potential outcome of his trials. While the state-level charges primarily focused on the murder and terrorism aspects of the case, the federal charges brought an entirely new dimension of legal complexity.

These charges, particularly the stalking and interstate murder allegations, carried much heavier penalties. If convicted, Mangione could face a life sentence in federal prison, which would likely far exceed the sentencing guidelines at the state level.

The involvement of federal prosecutors also signaled the seriousness with which the government viewed the case. The Obama-era reforms to anti-terrorism laws, coupled with the increase in federal involvement in domestic terror cases, meant that the charges brought against Mangione would not be taken lightly.

In many ways, Mangione's case became a flashpoint in the ongoing debate over domestic terrorism and the threat posed by ideologically motivated violence. Prosecutors were determined to set a precedent by showing that acts of violence, even those targeting corporate executives, could be prosecuted under federal law if they were motivated by political beliefs.

For Mangione's defense team, the federal charges created a significant challenge. Their argument that Mangione was suffering from mental illness and had acted out of a sense of moral outrage would have to contend with the federal government's characterization of his actions as deliberate and ideologically driven.

The defense argued that Mangione's mental health issues, such as depression and paranoia, should mitigate his responsibility for the murder, but federal prosecutors were unlikely to accept this defense, given the nature of his premeditated planning.

The broader implications of the federal charges were also felt outside the courtroom. Mangione became a focal point in discussions about the intersection of violence, ideology, and the healthcare system.

His case raised uncomfortable questions about how far an individual's dissatisfaction with a system can push them toward violent actions, and whether such actions could ever be justified under the guise of reform. Legal scholars and policymakers debated the extent to which Mangione's radicalization was a symptom of broader social issues, or whether it was simply the result of a lone individual's descent into extremism.

Ultimately, the federal charges complicated the legal proceedings, intensifying the public and media scrutiny of the case. The federal government's involvement would not only ensure that Mangione faced serious consequences for his actions but also set a precedent for how similar cases could be handled in the future.

As the trial progressed, it became increasingly clear that the fate of Luigi Mangione would not just affect his life but might have far-reaching implications for how the United States addresses the growing problem of domestic terrorism driven by political grievances.

CHAPTER FIVE

Healthcare in America: The Roots of Discontent

The murder of Brian Thompson by Luigi Mangione cannot be fully understood without addressing the larger societal context in which it occurred. The anger and frustration that fueled Mangione's actions were deeply intertwined with America's deeply flawed healthcare system.

For years, the country has grappled with rising healthcare costs, widespread insurance denials, and systemic inequities, all of which have left millions of Americans feeling trapped in a system that prioritizes profit over people.

The Deadly Shooting of Brian Thompson

While many individuals suffer quietly under the weight of medical debt and denied claims, Mangione's extreme act of violence thrust these issues into the national spotlight, shedding light on the immense frustration that many Americans feel toward an industry that has often seemed indifferent to their suffering.

This chapter will explore the roots of the discontent that led to the tragic events on December 4, 2023, with a focus on the high cost of healthcare in the United States, the devastating impact of denied insurance claims on families, and the role health insurance companies have played in fueling public anger and resentment.

Understanding the broader social and economic forces that shaped Mangione's worldview is essential for comprehending the violent act that shook the nation.

The High Cost of Healthcare in the U.S.

The United States has long been home to one of the most expensive healthcare systems in the world. Despite spending more per capita on healthcare than any other nation, the outcomes in terms of public health often lag behind other developed countries.

Americans face not only exorbitant costs for insurance premiums, deductibles, and out-of-pocket expenses, but they also experience a healthcare system that leaves many people underinsured or uninsured, often forcing them to choose between paying for basic necessities and receiving necessary medical treatment.

For decades, healthcare costs have steadily increased at a pace that outstrips inflation, with premiums rising faster than wages. This trend has created a profound sense of financial instability for many Americans, who find themselves unable to afford critical treatments, medications, and doctor's visits, even if they are insured.

According to data from the Centers for Medicare and Medicaid Services, healthcare spending in the U.S. reached nearly $4.1 trillion in 2020, making up 19.7% of the GDP. Yet despite these astronomical figures, access to quality care remains limited for millions, and disparities based on income, geography, and race continue to plague the system.

The cost of healthcare is often particularly burdensome for the middle class, who may earn too much to qualify for government assistance but too little to afford comprehensive coverage. In addition, the high cost of pharmaceuticals and hospital care has forced many families to go into debt, resulting in medical bills becoming one of the leading causes of bankruptcy in the country.

In a nation where healthcare is seen as a basic human right in many other parts of the world, the idea that it is treated as a commodity—a product to be bought and sold based on one's ability to pay—has fueled anger and resentment.

Luigi Mangione was one of many Americans who felt this frustration, but his story was not unique. The escalating cost of healthcare has been a driving force behind rising political discontent, as people across the country began to question why the richest nation in the world could not provide equitable healthcare to its citizens.

His actions were, in part, a manifestation of a deep-seated rage over a system that continuously leaves people vulnerable, despite their hard work and efforts to stay healthy.

The narrative that health insurance companies are designed to profit off human suffering only added to the frustration felt by Mangione and countless others. The astronomical cost of healthcare, combined with the systemic failures within the industry, created a combustible environment in which individuals like Mangione could feel increasingly alienated and powerless, even when the cost of healthcare was literally killing them.

Denied Claims and the Strain on Families

One of the most egregious aspects of America's healthcare system, and one of the primary grievances that Mangione voiced in his writings, was the practice of denying insurance claims.

The Deadly Shooting of Brian Thompson

Health insurance companies, which are supposed to act as a safety net for people in need, often find ways to refuse coverage for necessary treatments, procedures, or medications. This has had devastating consequences for families across the country who are left to grapple with both the emotional and financial toll of healthcare denial.

Denials are common for many reasons, ranging from technicalities and loopholes in policy language to outright disregard for medical necessity. For people struggling with chronic conditions, the threat of a denied claim can be a constant source of anxiety, as they depend on these claims to cover essential care.

Patients fighting cancer, heart disease, or other life-threatening illnesses often face multiple rounds of appeals, as insurance companies seek to reduce their payouts by denying coverage for critical treatments.

Mangione's own grievances with the insurance system were rooted in personal experiences, much like those of countless other Americans who have suffered due to insurance denials.

According to family members and acquaintances, Mangione had faced significant challenges when trying to access healthcare for himself and his loved ones. He had experienced the devastating impact of denied claims firsthand, and he believed that the insurance companies he so despised were intentionally putting profits over people's lives.

The emotional toll of being denied life-saving care can be overwhelming. Families already grappling with the physical, emotional, and financial strain of illness are then burdened by the added stress of trying to navigate an opaque and often indifferent system.

This frustration often turns into feelings of helplessness and despair, as patients and families realize that the bureaucratic systems are designed not to care for them, but to protect the interests of the corporations that run them.

The Deadly Shooting of Brian Thompson

Many families, like Mangione's, are forced to make impossible choices between paying for insurance premiums or putting food on the table. In some cases, families are driven into bankruptcy or forced to go without basic healthcare, despite having paid for insurance for years.

Mangione's deep anger toward the system was undoubtedly shaped by his personal experiences, but it also echoed the experiences of countless others who, like him, had been failed by the very system they relied on to stay healthy. His decision to take violent action was, in part, a response to this prolonged sense of injustice, exacerbated by years of systemic neglect.

The Role of Health Insurance Companies in Public Anger

At the heart of the public outrage over the healthcare system are the health insurance companies themselves. These corporations, often portrayed as profit-driven giants, have been at the center of growing resentment across the United States.

For many, health insurance companies are seen as the primary obstacle to receiving adequate care, and their policies—ranging from high premiums and deductibles to claim denials and pre-authorization requirements—have created a system that prioritizes profit over people's well-being.

Health insurance companies, like UnitedHealthcare, which was the company

Thompson led, have long been criticized for their role in driving up the cost of care and placing barriers between patients and the care they need.

These companies' emphasis on cost-cutting has often resulted in a push to limit care by denying claims, reducing reimbursement rates to doctors and hospitals, and requiring extensive pre-authorizations for treatments that doctors deem medically necessary. Insurance adjusters, who are often incentivized to deny claims in order to boost the company's bottom line, have become emblematic of the system's failings.

The insurance industry's practices are seen as inherently exploitative by many Americans, particularly those who have dealt with denied claims or insufficient coverage.

To many, it appears that the system is designed to profit from illness rather than to alleviate it. The public perception of insurance companies as faceless corporations, indifferent to human suffering, has contributed to the growing disillusionment with the healthcare system as a whole.

For individuals like Mangione, the actions of health insurance companies became a symbol of everything that was wrong with the system. His personal rage was compounded by a broader ideological belief that the healthcare system was rigged against the average person.

The Deadly Shooting of Brian Thompson

The executives who ran these companies, including Brian Thompson, came to represent an impersonal corporate machine that prioritized profits over people. Mangione's fixation on these figures, and his eventual decision to target Thompson, reflected the depth of the anger that many felt toward the growing consolidation of power within the healthcare industry.

As Mangione's case progressed, the role of health insurance companies became an inescapable focal point in the national conversation about the killing. While some saw Mangione's act as the result of one man's personal grievance, others viewed it as a symptom of a larger societal problem: a system in which individuals are left vulnerable to the whims of powerful, profit-driven corporations that have a monopoly on the health and well-being of millions.

For many Americans, the murder of Brian Thompson was a tragic and shocking event, but it also served as a stark reminder of the deep and persistent frustrations with the healthcare system. As the trial moved forward, the conversation about healthcare in America shifted, with more people beginning to question the fairness and accessibility of a system that had long been regarded as one of the most expensive and complex in the world.

In the wake of the tragedy, the outcry over the cost of healthcare, the pervasive practice of denied claims, and the role of health insurance companies in exacerbating these issues only grew louder.

Mangione's extreme act of violence, though tragic, had drawn attention to a crisis that millions of Americans were living through every day—a crisis that, for many, had gone unresolved for far too long.

CHAPTER SIX

Luigi Mangione's Motive: More Than a Murder

The tragic shooting of Brian Thompson, the CEO of UnitedHealthcare, was not simply the result of a spontaneous act of violence or a random act of hatred. Rather, it was the culmination of deep-rooted grievances that had been festering for years within Luigi Mangione.

The brutal assassination reflected not just personal resentment toward a corporate leader, but also a larger, more systematic frustration with the U.S. healthcare system—specifically, the practices of health insurance companies that many Americans, including Mangione, felt had caused undue suffering.

By examining Mangione's motives, it becomes clear that his violent actions were driven by a combination of personal experiences, ideological beliefs, and an overwhelming sense of injustice toward an industry he perceived as broken and indifferent to the needs of everyday people.

This chapter will explore Mangione's personal grievances with UnitedHealthcare, the writings found in his notebook that shed light on his views, and the broader philosophical and emotional framework behind his violent act.

Understanding Mangione's psyche and his distorted perception of justice will help explain why he believed that targeting Thompson—and, by extension, the healthcare system—was the only way to address the issues he had faced.

The Personal Grievance Against UnitedHealthcare

At the heart of Mangione's violent actions was a deep personal resentment against UnitedHealthcare, the health insurance giant where Brian Thompson served as CEO. For years, Mangione had struggled with the challenges posed by the U.S. healthcare system, and his frustrations were exacerbated by his interactions with UnitedHealthcare.

The Deadly Shooting of Brian Thompson

According to several sources close to Mangione, his family had been subjected to repeated denials of critical insurance claims. These denials were not for minor treatments, but for life-saving procedures and medications, leaving Mangione feeling powerless and betrayed by a system he believed was designed to exploit the vulnerable.

Mangione had long experienced the frustration of dealing with insurance companies that appeared more interested in protecting their bottom lines than in ensuring the well-being of their policyholders.

His resentment towards UnitedHealthcare began as a result of these personal experiences, where the bureaucracy of claims adjustments, the lack of transparency, and the impersonal nature of the company's decision-making process made him feel as if his family's health and financial stability were of no consequence.

The more Mangione dealt with these issues, the more he became convinced that the healthcare system, embodied by powerful insurers like UnitedHealthcare, was an enemy that needed to be confronted.

Thompson, as the CEO of UnitedHealthcare, symbolized to Mangione everything that was wrong with the industry. To Mangione, Thompson was not just a corporate executive; he was the face of an oppressive system that dictated the health and well-being of millions, yet denied them access to the very services they paid for.

The CEO of a company that denied claims, inflated premiums, and manipulated the system for financial gain became an enemy in Mangione's eyes, someone who represented the very forces that were holding people like him and his family hostage.

The level of personal grievance Mangione felt was evident in the way he meticulously planned the killing. For Mangione, this was not just a random act of violence; it was a calculated response to years of frustration and hardship, compounded by the sense of helplessness that so many others in similar situations experienced.

He believed that by eliminating Thompson, he would be striking a blow against a system that had left him and countless others in a state of despair.

The Writing Found in Mangione's Notebook

When police apprehended Mangione, they discovered a notebook in his possession that offered crucial insight into his motives and mindset. The notebook, filled with rambling thoughts and scrawled messages, revealed a clear ideological stance against the healthcare system and its corporate benefactors.

It was evident that Mangione had not simply targeted Thompson out of a momentary impulse but had carefully crafted a narrative in which he was positioned as a lone warrior fighting for justice against a faceless enemy.

One of the most telling passages in the notebook contained several harsh critiques of the healthcare system, including references to the suffering caused by insurance companies' refusal to cover necessary treatments.

Mangione wrote about the financial devastation that families like his had faced after having claims denied, and he expressed a sense of betrayal by the very institutions that were supposed to protect them. The tone of his writing was filled with anger, frustration, and a sense of helplessness, echoing the sentiments of many Americans who have felt similarly victimized by the healthcare industry.

In particular, Mangione's writings expressed a fervent belief that the healthcare system was designed to exploit the poor and middle class while enriching powerful executives and shareholders. He described the health insurance companies as "bloodsuckers," referring to them as entities that prey on the vulnerable for profit.

The notion that these companies would refuse to cover medical expenses to increase their profit margins was a major part of the narrative he constructed in his mind, which eventually led to the decision to target an individual at the very top of the healthcare hierarchy—Brian Thompson.

One chilling entry in the notebook read, "They want to control our lives, but I'll make them listen. The pain they caused is felt by millions, and I'll show them that no one is safe from their greed."

This passage, among others, revealed that Mangione saw his actions as part of a larger crusade—a mission to bring attention to the suffering caused by the healthcare system, with Thompson as the symbolic figurehead of everything that was wrong with it.

The writings revealed that Mangione did not see himself as a criminal or a murderer, but rather as a martyr—a person willing to sacrifice his freedom in order to ignite a conversation about the inequities of the healthcare system.

Understanding His View on the Healthcare System

To understand why Mangione believed that murdering Brian Thompson was justified, it is crucial to delve deeper into his worldview and his perception of the healthcare system. Mangione's view of the healthcare system was shaped by years of frustration with an industry that he believed was working against him at every turn.

As he saw it, health insurance companies were part of a larger machine that systematically denied care and exacerbated financial hardship for people who were already struggling with illness.

In Mangione's eyes, the healthcare system was not just inefficient—it was fundamentally broken. He believed that the executives who ran insurance companies, like Thompson, were disconnected from the realities of everyday people.

They made decisions based on data and profits, but they were completely unaware—or, in Mangione's view, indifferent—to the human cost of their decisions. The repeated denials, the rising premiums, and the manipulation of policies all contributed to a feeling of injustice that Mangione internalized. To him, the system wasn't just flawed—it was actively harming individuals like him.

In Mangione's mind, the murder of Thompson was not an act of random violence, but a calculated effort to strike at the heart of an industry that he saw as morally corrupt.

His belief in the righteousness of his cause was evident in his writings, where he referred to the "tyranny" of the healthcare industry and expressed his desire to "fight back" against the system that had caused so much pain. His violent actions were driven by the conviction that he was exposing the reality of the healthcare system to the world—a reality that, in his view, was hidden from the public eye by powerful corporate interests.

Mangione's extreme reaction was, in many ways, the result of a broader societal crisis—one in which millions of Americans feel that they are being crushed under the weight of a system that values profit over people.

While most people express their anger through protests, legal challenges, or advocacy, Mangione's frustration boiled over in the most violent and tragic way possible. His actions were, in his mind, a necessary response to a system that had repeatedly failed him and countless others.

The disillusionment that led him to murder Thompson was, ultimately, a reflection of the broader disillusionment many Americans feel toward a healthcare system that seems more concerned with making money than with saving lives.

The Deadly Shooting of Brian Thompson

By understanding Mangione's personal grievances, the writings found in his notebook, and his view of the healthcare system, we gain a clearer picture of the psychological and ideological forces that led him to commit murder.

While his actions were extreme and indefensible, they were deeply rooted in the very real frustrations felt by many Americans who believe that the healthcare system has abandoned them in favor of corporate interests. For Mangione, his crime was not just a personal vendetta—it was an attempt to ignite a broader conversation about healthcare reform, one that would bring attention to the issues that, in his mind, had been ignored for far too long.

CHAPTER SEVEN

Public Perception: From Villain to Folk Hero

The aftermath of Brian Thompson's murder sent shockwaves across the nation, sparking intense media coverage, debates on the state of the healthcare system, and the role of corporate leaders in perpetuating inequality.

As the case unfolded, an unexpected phenomenon began to take shape: Luigi Mangione, the man accused of assassinating the CEO of UnitedHealthcare, began to be portrayed not just as a criminal, but as a folk hero to a segment of the American public.

The Deadly Shooting of Brian Thompson

This chapter explores the transformation of Mangione's public image from that of a murderer to a symbol of defiance against an unjust system, driven in part by the support of a vocal group of protesters and the viral spread of the "Free Luigi" movement, particularly through social media.

This shift in perception is emblematic of how individuals, especially those who feel disenfranchised or oppressed, can turn to extreme actions and, in some cases, be celebrated as champions of a larger cause.

While Mangione's actions were undeniably violent and tragic, they tapped into a larger societal frustration—one rooted in the belief that the healthcare system, and by extension, powerful insurance companies like UnitedHealthcare, had grown far too powerful and were causing irreparable harm to individuals and families across the nation.

Understanding how Mangione became a symbol for some and a villain to others requires a look at the supporters who rallied behind him, the role of social media in amplifying his cause, and the underlying tactics used by the "Free Luigi" movement.

The Supporters Who Gathered Outside the Court

In stark contrast to the horror and tragedy of the murder itself, a small group of supporters gathered outside the Manhattan courthouse, holding placards and chanting slogans calling for Mangione's release.

These demonstrators, many of whom were strangers to Mangione, voiced their anger at healthcare companies and expressed solidarity with a man they saw as a victim of an unjust system. Some of the individuals in the crowd claimed personal experiences of being denied healthcare benefits or having family members suffer due to insurance denials.

For them, Mangione's act of violence, however extreme, was seen as a desperate attempt to fight back against a powerful and oppressive industry that had turned a blind eye to their suffering.

One of the most notable aspects of these demonstrations was the fervent passion of the protesters. They were not simply angry;

they were resolute, convinced that Mangione was not the sole person responsible for the tragedy, but that the system itself was the true villain.

Many of the placards carried by the supporters had slogans such as "End Healthcare Profiteering" and "UnitedHealthcare Is the Real Killer," highlighting the belief that the healthcare system, with its corporate-driven motives, was ultimately culpable for the pain and suffering of countless individuals.

For these protesters, the assassination of Brian Thompson became symbolic of the larger fight against systemic injustice in healthcare, and Mangione, in their eyes, was a martyr—someone who had sacrificed everything to shed light on a broken system.

This support was not limited to a small group of individuals. Reports indicated that the protests outside the courthouse began to grow in size as the case attracted more media attention. The fact that the demonstrators continued to chant slogans and wave signs in sub-zero temperatures showed their unwavering commitment to the cause.

This wasn't just a fleeting show of support; it was a growing movement fueled by a shared belief in the righteousness of Mangione's actions, albeit viewed through the lens of a morally complicated and polarizing issue.

The Deadly Shooting of Brian Thompson

The Role of Social Media in Glorifying Mangione

The case of Luigi Mangione quickly moved beyond the physical courtroom and streets of Manhattan and into the realm of social media, where it gained significant traction. Platforms like Twitter, Facebook, and Instagram were flooded with posts both condemning and defending Mangione.

The discourse surrounding the case began to evolve, with the most vocal defenders painting Mangione as a revolutionary figure who had taken radical action to challenge an industry that had failed to uphold its ethical obligations.

Hashtags like #FreeLuigi and #JusticeForLuigi began trending, especially among those who sympathized with the narrative that Mangione had been driven to extreme measures by the healthcare system's refusal to cover necessary medical expenses.

Social media posts shared graphic images of the protests, along with slogans, memes, and video clips that depicted Mangione's supporters as heroes fighting against an oppressive enemy. Many posts praised his bravery in challenging the system, with some likening him to historical figures who had taken drastic measures to bring attention to social injustice.

One popular tweet from an anonymous account read: "He may have taken a life, but the system he fought against has taken thousands. Maybe it's time we listen." This type of rhetoric was common in social media discussions, where Mangione was framed as a symbol of resistance rather than as a cold-blooded murderer.

Social media allowed for the rapid spread of this narrative, and the #FreeLuigi hashtag began to attract thousands of retweets and shares, amplifying the message that the true villain was not the man who pulled the trigger, but the faceless corporate structures that had caused widespread suffering.

The viral nature of social media gave Mangione's supporters a powerful tool to counter the negative press that often accompanies violent acts. In a sense, the rapid spread of the "Free Luigi" movement turned him into a symbol of the underdog, fighting back against the system with everything he had, even if it meant committing an extreme and unlawful act.

The quick spread of misinformation and skewed narratives in the form of memes, conspiracy theories, and viral videos made it easier for Mangione's actions to be seen in a more sympathetic light, allowing him to be framed as a martyr rather than a murderer.

The Tactics Behind the "Free Luigi" Movement

The "Free Luigi" movement was not just a passive expression of support for Mangione; it was a carefully orchestrated campaign designed to challenge the mainstream narrative and shift public opinion in his favor. Behind the scenes, anonymous figures or activists with a shared sense of disillusionment with the healthcare system began to strategize ways to elevate Mangione's cause.

Using social media platforms as their primary vehicle, they mobilized thousands of people to participate in virtual and physical protests, creating a groundswell of support for a man who had committed a brutal murder.

The tactics employed by these activists included organizing coordinated protests outside of courthouses and city centers, where demonstrators would gather and chant slogans demanding Mangione's release.

They also initiated crowdfunding campaigns to support legal costs and other expenses for Mangione's defense, as well as to fund continued protests and advocacy efforts. Some of these activists used their platforms to produce podcasts, videos, and blog posts, which focused not on the murder itself but on the larger issue of healthcare reform, with Mangione positioned as the face of this movement.

Another key tactic was the framing of Mangione as a victim of circumstance, rather than a deliberate killer. Many posts in the "Free Luigi" movement minimized the severity of his crime, instead emphasizing the systemic issues that led to his actions.

By focusing on the larger issue of healthcare inequality, these activists sought to draw attention away from the violent nature of the crime and instead highlight the reasons Mangione might have felt justified in his actions.

For many of Mangione's defenders, his act of violence was seen as the only way to force the public and media to confront a deeply flawed and exploitative healthcare system that had neglected the needs of millions of Americans for too long.

This campaign also drew from populist rhetoric, positioning Mangione as a "David against Goliath" figure—one man fighting against a massive, corrupt industry.

This narrative struck a chord with many Americans who were themselves frustrated with healthcare practices, such as high premiums, denied claims, and medical bankruptcies. The "Free Luigi" movement thus capitalized on the growing sense of dissatisfaction with the healthcare system, presenting Mangione as a hero who was willing to make the ultimate sacrifice for the cause.

In the eyes of many who supported Mangione, he was a symbol of resistance against an unjust system that had crushed the lives of ordinary people for too long. Whether or not the movement's tactics were effective in securing sympathy for Mangione, they undeniably created a powerful narrative that resonated with a significant portion of the population.

The question remained: how far would this sympathy extend? Would Mangione's actions ultimately be vindicated, or would the tragic nature of his crime overshadow the cause for which he claimed to stand?

Ultimately, the "Free Luigi" movement serves as a reflection of the deep-seated frustration and disillusionment that many Americans feel toward the healthcare system. While the movement might have been an extreme and controversial response to that frustration, it also highlighted the broader issues that continue to dominate discussions surrounding healthcare reform in the United States.

CHAPTER EIGHT

The Protest Movement: Healthcare Reform in the Spotlight

The murder of Brian Thompson, CEO of UnitedHealthcare, and the subsequent actions of Luigi Mangione became a tragic and controversial focal point for a broader societal conversation about healthcare in the United States.

While Mangione's supporters focused on his symbolic act of defiance against the healthcare industry, they also inadvertently sparked a nationwide debate that placed healthcare reform at the forefront of public discourse.

The Deadly Shooting of Brian Thompson

The rallying cry for healthcare justice, ignited by the protests surrounding Mangione's case, gave voice to millions of Americans who were angry, frustrated, and disillusioned with a system they believed had abandoned them.

The protest movement grew into a significant force, with protesters demanding not only justice for Mangione but also comprehensive reforms to ensure that healthcare served the needs of the many, not just the few.

In this chapter, we will explore how the shooting of Brian Thompson served as a catalyst for the broader healthcare reform movement, the voices of those oppressed by the system, and how the protests and public outcry transformed what was initially seen as a senseless act of violence into a rallying cry for change.

The Rallying Cry for Healthcare Justice

The shockwaves from the murder of Brian Thompson reverberated far beyond the courtroom and the immediate aftermath of the tragedy. As protesters rallied outside the courthouse, many began to see the event as more than just an isolated act of violence; they viewed it as a manifestation of the deep, systemic issues that plagued the American healthcare system.

The shooting became, in their eyes, the ultimate symbol of a healthcare system that prioritized profits over human lives, and for many, it became the spark that ignited a nationwide movement for healthcare justice.

The protests quickly grew in size and intensity, as more and more people took to the streets, advocating for change. The movement was not limited to just those who supported Mangione or agreed with his extreme tactics, but also included those who shared his frustrations and wanted to see a system that worked for everyone, not just the wealthy and powerful.

As the "Free Luigi" movement evolved, it became more about healthcare reform than about Mangione's specific case. The demands from protesters began to coalesce around key issues such as lowering healthcare costs, eliminating insurance company abuses, and increasing transparency and accountability in the industry.

The rallying cry for healthcare justice resonated with a broad spectrum of the population. People from all walks of life—patients who had faced medical bankruptcy, doctors who had been forced to navigate an increasingly complex and bureaucratic system, and activists who had long campaigned for healthcare reform—joined together in solidarity.

They recognized the underlying truth that the tragedy of Thompson's death was not an isolated incident, but rather a reflection of the larger, systemic failures of the healthcare industry.

The protests, while initially sparked by a specific act of violence, quickly evolved into a powerful movement calling for sweeping reforms that would address the root causes of the frustration many people felt.

One of the key demands of the protest movement was a shift in the way healthcare was delivered in the U.S. Specifically, many protesters called for a universal healthcare system that would ensure access to care for all Americans, regardless of their income or status.

They argued that a single-payer system would remove the profit-driven motives of insurance companies and ensure that healthcare decisions were based on patient needs rather than financial considerations.

This demand, though contentious and far from universally accepted, became a central theme of the nationwide debate that Mangione's actions had helped to catalyze.

Voices of the Oppressed: Testimonials from Protesters

As the protest movement grew, so too did the voices of the oppressed—the individuals and families whose lives had been upended by the failures of the healthcare system.

Many of these voices came from those who had experienced firsthand the devastating effects of insurance companies' refusal to cover necessary treatments, who had lost loved ones due to delays or denials of care, or who had been forced into financial ruin because of astronomical medical bills.

These testimonials painted a vivid picture of a broken system that had failed to live up to its promise of providing care to those in need.

One powerful story came from Natalie Monarrez, a Staten Island resident who had lost both her mother and her savings due to denied insurance claims. Monarrez shared her story at a rally in support of Mangione, saying, "My mother was denied coverage for a life-saving treatment that would have extended her life.

Instead, we watched her suffer, unable to pay for the care she desperately needed. My family lost everything trying to fight the insurance companies. I feel like we were pushed to the edge, and so I understand why someone like Luigi would take such drastic action." Her words resonated with many in the crowd, as they mirrored the frustrations of millions who felt they had been wronged by the system.

Similarly, the voice of Mark Rodriguez, a former healthcare worker who had seen the industry from the inside, echoed the same sentiments. "I worked in insurance for over a decade. I saw firsthand how people's lives were ruined because of the decisions made by people like Brian Thompson.

But what we don't see in the headlines are the people who are stuck in a system that doesn't care about them. Those of us in the trenches, we knew something had to change. But we didn't know it would take something as drastic as this to finally get people's attention."

For these individuals, Mangione's actions were seen not as a senseless murder, but as a desperate cry for help—an attempt to bring attention to the real, lived consequences of a healthcare system that many believed had failed them.

They argued that, although the manner in which Mangione sought to make his point was violent and tragic, it was driven by a deeper need to draw attention to the ongoing struggles of ordinary Americans who had been fighting against a system that seemed indifferent to their pain.

The voices of these protesters and advocates helped humanize the larger movement for healthcare justice, giving it a personal, emotional context that resonated with millions across the country.

How the Shooting Sparked a Nationwide Debate

The events surrounding Brian Thompson's murder and the subsequent protests did not occur in a vacuum. They were part of a broader national conversation about healthcare reform that had been brewing for years, especially in the wake of the passage of the Affordable Care Act (ACA) and the ongoing debates about its effectiveness.

While the ACA had expanded access to healthcare for millions of Americans, it had also exposed deep divides within the country over how healthcare should be provided and funded. The frustrations expressed by Mangione's supporters reflected a broader disillusionment with the healthcare system, and the shooting itself was seen by some as a tragic, albeit extreme, expression of this dissatisfaction.

As the protests spread across the nation, they sparked a heated debate in the media and in the halls of Congress. Political pundits, activists, and policymakers weighed in, with some condemning Mangione's actions as an act of terrorism, while others saw it as a symptom of a broken system in need of urgent reform.

The Deadly Shooting of Brian Thompson

The debate over the future of healthcare in America intensified, with many calling for a complete overhaul of the system, including a push for Medicare for All—a policy proposal that would create a single-payer healthcare system for all Americans.

The debate also sparked questions about the morality of the healthcare system itself. Many asked whether it was right for insurance companies to have so much power over the lives and health of ordinary citizens.

Could a system that allowed for profits to be made at the expense of people's health really be justified? And if such a system was inherently flawed, what were the ethical implications of people resorting to violence in order to get the attention of policymakers and the public?

In Washington, the protests did not go unnoticed. Lawmakers on both sides of the political spectrum began to reassess their positions on healthcare reform. Some, particularly progressives, saw the protests as a call to action, urging them to push harder for policies that would curb the influence of insurance companies and create a more equitable system.

Others, more conservative lawmakers, viewed the protests with suspicion and as an indication of the growing unrest among the electorate. Some called for stricter penalties for those who participated in violent acts in the name of social justice, while others worried about the potential for similar acts of violence in the future.

At the same time, healthcare reform advocacy groups saw a surge in support, as new voices joined the fight for change. These groups seized the opportunity to push their agenda, using the tragedy of Thompson's murder as a platform to argue for a radical transformation of the healthcare system. In many ways, the shooting and the protests that followed provided an unexpected but powerful catalyst for the larger conversation about the future of healthcare in the U.S.

The movement for healthcare justice that grew out of the tragedy of Brian Thompson's murder was not a monolithic force, nor was it without controversy. But it undeniably brought the issue of healthcare reform to the forefront of the national consciousness, challenging the country to confront its systemic failures and reconsider the direction of its healthcare policies.

As protests continued and the debate deepened, it became clear that the tragedy had forced Americans to rethink their approach to healthcare—perhaps forever.

CHAPTER NINE

Brian Thompson's Legacy: A Father's Impact

The murder of Brian Thompson, CEO of UnitedHealthcare, shocked the nation and sent ripples through the healthcare industry. While the immediate focus of the media and public was on the brutal nature of his death and the motives behind it, the legacy of Brian Thompson extends far beyond the tragedy of his assassination.

In the wake of his death, both his family and the larger healthcare landscape were left to grapple with the personal and professional consequences of his passing.

In this chapter, we will explore the life and career of Brian Thompson, his significant role at UnitedHealthcare, and the far-reaching impact of his untimely death on his family, colleagues, and the healthcare industry at large.

The Life and Career of Brian Thompson

Brian Thompson was not just a corporate executive; he was a man who had devoted much of his life to shaping one of the largest healthcare organizations in the world. Born and raised in the United States, Thompson had a career that spanned decades, during which he honed his skills in business leadership and corporate strategy.

His educational background and early career were marked by a strong focus on economics and business, laying the foundation for his eventual rise to the top ranks of the healthcare industry.

Thompson's career trajectory within the healthcare industry was both impressive and purposeful. His ability to navigate complex challenges and his knack for strategic thinking helped him ascend through various roles at UnitedHealthcare, ultimately culminating in his position as CEO.

At the time of his death, Thompson was widely regarded as a forward-thinking executive with a deep understanding of the healthcare landscape. His leadership was seen as key to UnitedHealthcare's growth and ability to manage the complex issues facing the industry, including rising healthcare costs, insurance coverage, and regulatory pressures.

Throughout his career, Thompson was a polarizing figure. For some, he represented the face of a rapidly consolidating and increasingly profitable healthcare sector, leading a company that served millions but was often criticized for its handling of claims, patient care, and administrative practices.

For others, Thompson was a leader committed to improving the accessibility and affordability of healthcare, working tirelessly to steer his company through the storm of a turbulent and highly scrutinized industry. His leadership style, characterized by ambition and pragmatism, made him both a respected and controversial figure within the healthcare world.

Thompson was known for his sharp business acumen, but he was also a deeply committed father and family man. He was married with two children, and those who knew him personally described him as a loving and supportive father, deeply involved in his family's lives despite the demands of his high-profile career.

His death, which occurred on the morning of December 4, 2023, left a profound emotional void in the lives of his family, friends, and colleagues.

The loss of such an influential figure also raised questions about the future direction of UnitedHealthcare and the larger healthcare industry, especially considering the ongoing debate about the power of insurance companies and the struggles of ordinary Americans to access affordable care.

Thompson's Role at UnitedHealthcare

Brian Thompson's position at UnitedHealthcare was one of immense responsibility and influence. As CEO, he was not only the public face of the company but also a key decision-maker who guided the company through some of the most challenging periods in healthcare history. UnitedHealthcare, one of the largest health insurance companies in the world, has over

50 million customers across the U.S. and plays a significant role in shaping the healthcare landscape.

Thompson's role at UnitedHealthcare was marked by both achievements and controversies. On one hand, he led the company through an era of rapid expansion, overseeing a series of mergers, acquisitions, and partnerships that increased the company's market share and solidified its position as an industry leader.

Under his leadership, UnitedHealthcare increased its presence in both the private and public healthcare sectors, working with government programs such as Medicaid and Medicare, in addition to its private insurance offerings. His efforts to streamline operations and reduce costs were seen as critical to the company's bottom line.

On the other hand, UnitedHealthcare—and Thompson, by extension—faced significant criticism over the company's business practices. As insurance premiums continued to rise, many consumers and advocacy groups accused UnitedHealthcare and other insurers of prioritizing profit over patient care.

One of the main points of contention was the practice of denying claims, particularly for high-cost treatments and life-saving procedures, which created an environment where patients were often left without the care they desperately needed.

Thompson's leadership was often scrutinized for its role in overseeing these practices, and while he worked to improve customer satisfaction in certain areas, the company remained the subject of intense public scrutiny.

Thompson's leadership extended beyond just financial concerns. He was involved in several initiatives aimed at improving health outcomes, especially in underprivileged communities. UnitedHealthcare, under his guidance, invested in programs designed to reduce health disparities, improve access to preventive care, and support the broader public health infrastructure.

While these initiatives were often praised by healthcare professionals and some policymakers, they were not without their critics, who argued that the company was more focused on corporate image than on meaningful reform.

In the wake of his death, Thompson's legacy at UnitedHealthcare has been the subject of significant debate. For many within the company, his passing represented the end of an era—a period of stability and growth that had solidified UnitedHealthcare's dominance in the marketplace.

However, for those who felt that the healthcare system was stacked against patients and working families, Thompson's death became a symbol of the entrenched interests of powerful healthcare executives who, they believed, were complicit in a system that prioritized profit over people.

The Impact of His Death on His Family and the Healthcare Industry

The emotional toll of Thompson's murder was immediate and far-reaching, affecting not only his family but also the broader healthcare community. For his wife and two children, the loss was both personal and devastating.

The death of a father and husband left a void in their lives that could never be filled, and the public nature of the tragedy only added to the emotional strain. While Thompson's legacy as a businessman was complex, for his family, he was simply a loving father who had worked tirelessly to provide for them.

The impact of his death also reverberated within UnitedHealthcare. The company, which had always prided itself on its leadership, found itself grappling with the sudden loss of its CEO, and there was widespread concern about how the company would move forward without Thompson at the helm.

In the wake of the tragedy, some speculated that Thompson's death could lead to a period of instability at UnitedHealthcare, potentially affecting its operations and business dealings. The company was forced to address not only the personal loss of a respected leader but also the ongoing scrutiny it faced over its business practices.

The broader healthcare industry, too, was forced to confront the implications of Thompson's death. His passing highlighted the tension between corporate interests and the public outcry over the rising costs of healthcare and the perceived greed of insurance companies.

For many, Thompson's death symbolized the larger issue of an industry that often seemed more concerned with its profit margins than with the people it was supposed to serve. As the news of his death spread, the healthcare industry was once again thrust into the spotlight, with renewed calls for reform and a reevaluation of the role that powerful corporations like UnitedHealthcare play in shaping the future of American healthcare.

At the same time, Thompson's death has also contributed to a broader narrative that emphasizes the need for greater accountability within the healthcare industry. Critics of UnitedHealthcare, including activists, healthcare professionals, and policy advocates, saw his death as a stark reminder of the deep inequities within the system.

His passing, while tragic, has served as a rallying cry for those pushing for sweeping reforms that would make healthcare more accessible, affordable, and patient-centered.

In conclusion, Brian Thompson's legacy is a complex one—marked by both professional success and controversy. His life and career were deeply intertwined with the fate of UnitedHealthcare and the larger healthcare landscape.

While his death has had a profound impact on his family, colleagues, and the healthcare industry, it has also catalyzed a broader conversation about the state of healthcare in America. Whether as a symbol of corporate success or as the face of a deeply flawed system, Thompson's legacy will continue to shape the ongoing debate about healthcare reform for years to come.

CHAPTER TEN

The Larger Implications: Terrorism, Politics, and Healthcare

The tragic death of Brian Thompson, the CEO of UnitedHealthcare, at the hands of Luigi Mangione has sparked a national conversation that extends far beyond the individual case. As the legal process unfolds, the case raises important questions about the definition of terrorism, the intersection of healthcare policy and public sentiment, and the potential for broader political and legal consequences.

This chapter examines the larger implications of the case, analyzing how Mangione's actions challenge legal and societal norms, the future of healthcare reform in the U.S., and the potential shifts in legal precedents regarding terrorism and corporate accountability.

The Definition of Terrorism in Mangione's Case

One of the most significant aspects of Luigi Mangione's prosecution is the inclusion of terrorism charges. While the nature of his crime—assassinating a corporate executive—might seem an isolated act of violence, the implications are much broader, as it is framed as an attack designed to influence the healthcare system at large.

Federal prosecutors have charged Mangione with murder and terrorism, arguing that his actions were intended not only to kill

Thompson but also to intimidate the public and force a reexamination of healthcare policy.

The use of terrorism charges in this case represents a nuanced approach to defining terrorism within the context of domestic acts of violence aimed at disrupting societal systems. Traditionally, terrorism is associated with politically motivated violence, often linked to ideologies or groups with specific political agendas.

However, in Mangione's case, the charges reflect a shift in how terrorism is defined in the legal realm—now encompassing acts that target the integrity of a system that governs public welfare, such as the healthcare sector.

Legal experts have pointed out that this case sets a dangerous precedent, as it brings corporate leaders and powerful institutions into the crosshairs of terrorism laws. If Mangione is convicted under these charges, it could set a legal precedent for labeling other acts of violence against corporate figures, particularly those in sectors such as finance, healthcare, or energy, as terrorism.

Such a ruling could embolden efforts to expand counter-terrorism measures to include individual acts of violence aimed at influencing public policy. This would change the legal landscape and redefine how acts of violence are prosecuted in the context of corporate and political dissent.

The Deadly Shooting of Brian Thompson

At the heart of the debate is the question of whether Mangione's grievances against UnitedHealthcare and the broader healthcare industry justify his resorting to violence.

Some critics argue that his actions were a violent expression of frustration against a system that fails to address the real needs of patients, while others warn that it is dangerous to validate acts of terrorism driven by personal grievances, no matter how legitimate they might seem in the eyes of the perpetrator.

Ultimately, the legal classification of Mangione's actions could lead to a broader reconsideration of what constitutes terrorism in a modern context, especially as it pertains to political dissent, corporate power, and public safety.

Healthcare Policy Reform: What's Next?

Beyond the legal ramifications, the shooting of Brian Thompson and the subsequent events have thrust the issue of healthcare reform into the national spotlight. As public protests and demonstrations erupt across the country, many are asking: what's next for healthcare policy in the U.S.?

The debate over the rising cost of healthcare, the denial of claims, and the perceived greed of insurance companies has reached a boiling point. In the wake of Thompson's murder, there is a growing demand for systemic reform that addresses the needs of ordinary Americans who feel increasingly powerless in the face of monopolistic health insurance practices.

Mangione's actions, although extreme and criminal, have acted as a catalyst, forcing the conversation on healthcare to the forefront of political discourse.

For some, the case serves as a wake-up call, highlighting the urgent need for comprehensive reform in the U.S. healthcare system. The rising costs of premiums, co-pays, and out-of-pocket expenses have left millions of Americans struggling to afford necessary care.

Simultaneously, the practice of denying claims or providing insufficient coverage for patients has left countless individuals unable to access life-saving treatments, creating a growing sense of frustration with the system. In light of these concerns, the murder of Brian Thompson has given voice to an anger that has been simmering beneath the surface for years.

Healthcare reform advocates are calling for a range of changes to ensure that healthcare is more affordable, accessible, and patient-centered. Among the most prominent proposals are calls for a universal healthcare system, such as Medicare for All, which would ensure that every American has access to healthcare regardless of their ability to pay.

Supporters of this approach argue that a single-payer system would remove the profit motive from healthcare and allow doctors and medical professionals to focus on patient care rather than financial considerations.

Others are advocating for stronger regulation of insurance companies, including limits on premiums and co-pays, and stricter oversight of how insurance companies deny or delay claims. The hope is that greater transparency in the claims process and a reduction in the power of insurers would help ensure that patients are not left to navigate an opaque and often adversarial system when they need care the most.

However, any major shift in healthcare policy will likely face significant opposition from the powerful healthcare and insurance industries, which will continue to lobby against sweeping reforms that could cut into their profits. The murder of Brian Thompson has reignited the debate, but it is still unclear whether it will result in tangible change in the short term.

As public opinion continues to evolve, healthcare reform is expected to remain a major issue in U.S. politics, with political leaders on both sides of the aisle forced to respond to the public's growing discontent. This case will undoubtedly continue to shape the national dialogue on healthcare in the years to come, influencing everything from legislative priorities to presidential campaigns.

Legal Precedents and How This Case Could Reshape Future Prosecutions

The legal implications of the Mangione case extend beyond the charges themselves. The way this case unfolds in the courts could set a precedent for how similar cases involving corporate leaders, violence, and political motives are handled in the future. The inclusion of terrorism charges, in particular, is groundbreaking, as it could influence how future cases involving domestic violence and political dissent are prosecuted.

Historically, acts of violence motivated by political or ideological beliefs have been prosecuted as terrorism, but the definition of terrorism has traditionally been limited to actions taken by organized groups or those with a clearly articulated agenda.

In Mangione's case, however, the charges indicate a shift in how terrorism might be defined in the context of individual actors and personal grievances. The outcome of this case could impact how the justice system approaches cases that involve lone actors attempting to influence policy or public opinion through violent means.

Additionally, the case could have a lasting effect on the way corporate figures are protected from acts of violence motivated by public anger or dissatisfaction. In recent years, corporate executives and leaders have become increasingly vulnerable to public scrutiny, and acts of violence against them, while rare, have occurred with increasing frequency.

If Mangione is convicted of terrorism, it may lead to greater legal protections for corporate leaders and an expanded interpretation of what constitutes an act of terror in the context of corporate power and political dissent.

Moreover, the Mangione case could set the stage for future legal battles over the intersection of violence, politics, and corporate responsibility. The notion that corporate leaders might be held accountable, in part, for the consequences of their companies' actions could shape future prosecutions, especially if violence is deemed a response to corporate behavior.

This case may spur new conversations about the legal and moral responsibilities of corporations, their leaders, and their role in shaping public policy.

In conclusion, the murder of Brian Thompson by Luigi Mangione has far-reaching implications that extend beyond the immediate legal proceedings. The case raises questions about the definition of terrorism, the future of healthcare reform, and the broader political landscape in the U.S.

As the case progresses, it will continue to shape public debates on healthcare, corporate power, and the use of violence to challenge perceived injustices, potentially influencing legal precedents and social movements for years to come.

CONCLUSION

Reflection on the Tragedy and Its Consequences

The tragic assassination of Brian Thompson by Luigi Mangione has stirred a national reckoning that extends far beyond the immediate shock of the event itself. This tragedy has brought issues of healthcare reform, the power of corporate interests, and the nature of violence as a tool for political change to the forefront of the American consciousness.

As the legal proceedings continue and public sentiment evolves, the case serves as both a symbol of the deep frustrations within the U.S. healthcare system and a stark reminder of the consequences of failing to address systemic injustices.

The murder of Brian Thompson was a senseless act of violence that resulted in the loss of a life, a family's grief, and the disruption of a major corporation in the heart of the U.S. healthcare industry. Thompson's death, while tragic in its own right, has become emblematic of the larger societal tensions that have been simmering for years within the American healthcare system.

His role as the CEO of UnitedHealthcare placed him at the intersection of two conflicting realities: one in which he worked to lead a global corporation that served millions of patients, and another where his company was vilified by a growing portion of the public who viewed it as part of the problem—the corporate profiteering in an industry that they believe has failed them.

For those directly affected by the actions of healthcare giants like UnitedHealthcare, Thompson's death has underscored a deep-rooted distrust of the system. For them, the tragedy is not just the loss of a corporate leader, but a manifestation of the pain they feel from years of struggling against high medical bills, denied insurance claims, and a healthcare system that often seems more concerned with profits than patients.

In this sense, Mangione's actions, though extreme, reflect the anger and frustration felt by many Americans who have been disenfranchised by a system that appears to prioritize corporate interests over the health and well-being of individuals.

But while the emotional and psychological toll of this tragedy is undeniable, it is important to reflect on the larger consequences of this event. The question remains: how can this moment of violence be transformed into a force for change?

The focus on healthcare reform, inspired by the shooting and the outpouring of support for Mangione, has opened a wider dialogue, but it also serves as a painful reminder of the limits of violence in addressing systemic issues.

This tragedy, while a catalyst for debate, cannot be seen as a legitimate solution to the problem of healthcare inequality. Rather, it serves as a grim symbol of the need for real, substantive change that comes from thoughtful and peaceful reform efforts, not from bloodshed and terror.

Moving Forward: The Fight for Healthcare Justice

While the case of Luigi Mangione is a stark reminder of the deep dissatisfaction that exists within the U.S. healthcare system, it also points to the ongoing fight for healthcare justice. For years, activists, policy makers, and citizens have been calling for changes to the system to ensure that healthcare is accessible and affordable for all Americans, regardless of their income, race, or location.

The events surrounding Thompson's death have only intensified these calls, with many Americans viewing his assassination as a moment of reckoning.

Moving forward, the question becomes how best to address the systemic issues that contributed to the dissatisfaction and anger felt by Mangione and others like him. The current system of private insurance, coupled with astronomical medical costs, has left millions of Americans vulnerable and frustrated. Reform is necessary, and it is clear that action must be taken to address these inequities.

Healthcare justice movements, from advocates for Medicare for All to those calling for stronger protections for consumers against insurance companies, have found renewed energy in the aftermath of this tragedy.

The death of Brian Thompson has reignited a national conversation about the flaws in the system—especially as it pertains to insurance companies' practices of denying claims, charging high premiums, and favoring profits over care.

To truly move forward, meaningful policy reform must focus on making healthcare a fundamental right for all citizens. This could include expanding public health insurance options, introducing price controls for medical procedures and prescription drugs, and implementing greater transparency in medical billing.

Furthermore, the healthcare industry must be held accountable for its role in perpetuating inequality. Corporations like UnitedHealthcare cannot continue to operate in ways that prioritize profits over people's well-being. The system needs to shift away from a model driven by profits and focus on patient care, which requires government oversight, consumer protections, and robust advocacy for those who need it most.

While the tragic loss of Brian Thompson may act as a catalyst for change, it is imperative that the movement toward healthcare reform be driven by peaceful, constructive efforts. Change must come through legislation, public engagement, and collective action, not through violence.

The death of a man, no matter the circumstances, should never be seen as a legitimate tool for bringing about change. But in the aftermath of this tragedy, we are reminded of how dire the need for change is, and how crucial it is to address the problems of healthcare accessibility and affordability in ways that promote healing, not harm.

The Continuing Debate: Can True Change Come from Violence?

One of the most difficult questions raised by the events surrounding Brian Thompson's death is whether violence can ever truly lead to meaningful change. The murder of Thompson by Luigi Mangione has become a focal point for debates about the efficacy of violence as a means of addressing political or social grievances.

While there is no doubt that Mangione's actions have brought attention to the issues within the healthcare system, the manner in which he chose to voice his discontent—through an act of terror—raises serious moral and ethical concerns.

In the wake of this tragedy, there are those who view Mangione as a hero, a man who took drastic action to draw attention to the flaws in the healthcare system. For some, his actions represent the culmination of years of pent-up frustration with a system that has denied them care, left them drowning in medical debt, and forced them to fight against an impersonal bureaucracy.

These individuals, many of whom feel as though they have been abandoned by both the healthcare system and their government, might see Mangione's violent act as a necessary evil—an extreme measure taken to bring about necessary change. In their eyes, the death of Thompson is a form of retribution, a consequence of the oppressive nature of the healthcare system that they feel has done more harm than good.

However, the vast majority of people, even those who sympathize with the underlying grievances that motivated Mangione, reject the notion that violence can be a justifiable means of change. History has shown that while violence may lead to short-term attention or upheaval, it rarely produces lasting, meaningful reform.

Instead, it often results in further polarization, retaliation, and the perpetuation of cycles of violence. While it is true that acts of violence can raise awareness and force difficult conversations to the surface, they cannot fundamentally address the structural problems that require systemic solutions.

True and lasting change in healthcare—and in society as a whole—must come from dialogue, negotiation, and reform, not from acts of terror. The fight for healthcare justice will not be won through violence, but through collective action that puts pressure on lawmakers, corporate leaders, and public officials to prioritize the well-being of individuals over profits.

The challenge moving forward is to ensure that the anger and frustration felt by so many Americans are channeled into peaceful and effective movements that push for reforms that can make a real difference in people's lives.

In conclusion, the assassination of Brian Thompson by Luigi Mangione is a tragedy that has left a lasting impact on both the healthcare industry and the broader national conversation about the future of healthcare in the United States.

The Deadly Shooting of Brian Thompson

While it has undoubtedly sparked renewed interest in healthcare justice, it has also raised uncomfortable questions about the nature of political violence and its role in shaping societal change.

As we reflect on the events that have transpired, it is crucial to remember that while the issues at the heart of this case are real and deserving of attention, true change must come through peaceful, democratic means—reform driven by empathy, justice, and a commitment to the public good.

www.ingramcontent.com/pod-product-compliance
Lightning Source LLC
LaVergne TN
LVHW020845190125
801452LV00037B/677